The Tin Trailer

and other poems for the hurting and the hopeful

By Lorene Masters

Author Acknowledgment

Thank you

To Darcy Stafford and Kim Buszko for the inspiration.

To my sister Connie, who has always been there.

To Mr. Robert Timberman, my seventh-grade English teacher, who believed in me when no one else did.

To my husband Dave and our two girls, Hannah and Rachel—you've shown me what true love is.

To all the wonderful and talented people who contributed photos and illustrations.

Most of all, I want to thank my Lord and Savior Jesus Christ for allowing me the emotions and granting me the words to express them.

Dedicated to my mother.

Irene Weisbrod Meland
1922 -1988

Preface

To be human means to experience pain. Loss and the inevitable grief that follows can leave us feeling empty and alone. Whether it's the passing away of a loved one, the dismissal from a job, the altering of our physical health, the move to a new location or the ending of a significant relationship, we all sooner or later will know what it's like to have a broken heart.

The death of anyone or anything that meant something to us hurts. Our grief can wear the face of anger and despair one minute and hope and healing the next. All the grief experts say that it's best to express, not repress, our feelings. How do we do this?

Can God handle our anger?

Our questions? Our tears?

Yes to all of the above. God cares and is well acquainted with our emotions wherever they may find us. Grief is universal. It's a tunnel that we pass through and hopefully emerge from filled with optimism and wisdom for tomorrow.

The greatest grief I felt to date was when my mother died in 1988. But I also hurt for the death of my two-month-old niece Isabel, my cat Sabrina that I had to give away, and the exhilarating and often relentless misery of unrequited love. I wrote about these and other firsthand experiences. Also included are poems about the pain I imagine one must feel from having an abortion, losing a spouse, a child who's been abducted, a betrayal of marriage vows, and other agonizing, real life situations. In the following pages, I pray that you will find comfort in knowing that you are not alone—that there is renewal beyond your pain and that there is hope. There is always hope because God who has suffered as we do desires for us to heal and will help us every step of the way.

"Earth has no sorrow that Heaven cannot heal."

Thomas Moore

I Remember Momma

I remember Momma as a mother remembers her child.
As the dry earth remembers the rain in the hot summertime.

I remember Momma as the river flows silently
down where memories lay quietly sleeping.

I remember Momma as my hands hold the purple lilacs,
freshly picked for her, hoping to find her where my heart
remembers her to be.
Home with a love-laced vase ready to receive.

Shattered glass.
Broken heart.
Love rejected.

If I looked long and hard enough I could probably find the strength to purchase a new vase but never a new Momma.

I'll make due to hold the flowers in my hands until my
heart can rest at the sight of her.

Now and forever the purple lilacs are for Momma
because she's loved and missed very much.

"Love is as strong as death."

Song of Solomon 8:6

photos by Rachel Masters

Remembering

Yesterday, life was as I was, young and simple.
When did all the confusion start?
Was it when I realized that Raggedy Ann
Was just a bag full of rags?
Or when I gave up hopscotch because I had to
Remove my high heels?
I would love to go back.
If only I could find Raggedy Ann.

For Mother

Snowy prisoners of stone,
Life in my mother as we knew it,
Is gone.
Memories flood in trickles, then waves.
Washing over me, drowning me.

Love, oh for sweet love of Mother.
In Him love and life are eternal.

Memories fade.
Laughter lingers.
Joy is king.

His Spirit cannot be kept in a body no longer alive.
His Spirit is the life now gone back to be with Him forever.

I touch her cement-like face.
Cold.
Hard.

Her hair soft as spring earth buried for new life to grow in.
I take some to remember its rich color for it is winter now
And all I have are the memories of how it felt when I touched in the springtime.

Her hands are chilled upon her stiff body.
I kiss them, then her lips.
She smiles, watching from above.
She is happier now than she has ever been.
Her spirit dances with me and us with Jesus.

I look at her, seeing not her but the ultimate answer to my greatest prayer, eternal rest, no more pain.

Young again, the same age as me,
Wearing a gray dress, sitting in a lilac field.
The scent of flowers is the scent of God.
Street of gold; God the only light needed.

Snow crunches. Bodies in brown boots lower the
Rose-colored, white laced package that His Spirit
Lived in deep into the frozen ground.
Icy snow fell. Hearts were warm and bleeding.
Ashes to ashes, dust to dust.

I look up, knowing that she is not there but with Him.
And He cannot remain a snowy prisoner of stone.
For with Him, love and life are eternal.

"I am the resurrection and the life. He who believes in
me though he may die, he shall live."

John 11:25

photo by Rachel Masters

Please Someone Cry with Me

Please someone, cry with me.
I am so tired of crying alone.
I know that you cannot change what has happened—
Cannot bring my mother back.
I would not ask that of you.
But, please, if you've got the time, cry with me.
I am so tired of crying alone.

He said to comfort those who mourn
And weep with those who weep.
As He Himself wept at the painful morn of
The passing of one so loved.
He said that we are to be like Him,
That we are to die with Him.
I think dying means crying with those who are broken inside.
So, if you've got the time and the wisdom to leave your fancy words behind, come along and feel His heart and cry with those who are feeling His death.

"Rejoice with those who rejoice and weep with those who weep."

Romans 12:15

photo by Christina Fuhr

Some Days

Some days my eyes look so hard for Momma.
They walk the street that she lived on.
They see the love that would always meet me at the door.
They feel the warmth of her heart.
Then rejected by reality, they cry and cry.

For she is not there, and it keeps snowing and snowing
On all the pretty flowers that she planted for me
In her front yard.

I shiver in the sun.
My eyes bleed upon the foot of snow that has covered her grave this spring.

Where have the lilacs gone that she loved so much?
Gone like the scent of Moonwind she loved to wear.
Where are the swing sets and sand boxes?
The mother who would forever be there in pedal pushers
And yellow curlers almost like being one of us as we laughed and played.

Where has she gone?
She was always there in the sticker-filled garden that I hated to work in or in the kitchen
Canning food that I loved to eat.
Why did the wind have to blow and bring this change?
This shock to my heart? Why can't I find her anywhere?

I miss you, Momma.
Did you know that you would leave voids that could not
Be filled with anyone or anything?

Please, Jesus, hear my cry amongst the noisy laughter of life.
Fill me with Your comfort and eternal love.
I can see the blood-tears You shed for me.
Hold me tight until the day I can see Momma again
When we reign together with You.

For Those Who Know Him

For those who know Him
Death is the glad hello of tomorrows.
It's the waking of life as life is meant to be.
It's the drying of the tears of the child
And the rejoicing of the mother.

It's the long, cold nights
Of longing and weeping,
Heavy heart broken,
Coming to an end.

For those who know Him
Death is hope fulfilled,
Darkness conquered by Light.
Body redeemed from sin.
Resurrected in Him
To sorrow no more.

Dreams

The shortest route to you is through the garden of dreams.
The noise of the lady upstairs, laughing, talking, loving mother.

The quietness of your breathing as you rest,
The pleasure as you wake and we pray together,
Comforted by love and at least one last touch.

The joy when He finally comes in the clouds for me.
The marketplace will be emptied,
No more hungry people begging for bread.

The hope of seeing Him and knowing that you are with Him.
Safe.
Soon, so soon, I shall wake and know.

Photo by Dave Masters

My Best Friend

Surely,
He has not forgotten me but I have forgotten Him,
My best friend.
The one who gave me the heart to dream when hope was dim,
The strength to wait, the smiles to get me through.

Surely,
He is the same.
I have changed, walked out the door.
Angry.
He never moved from the room.
Was never uncomfortable as He waited for me to return
To come back inside to Him.
He knew that my hands would get cold holding onto
Frozen doorknobs that weren't meant to be opened by me.

Surely,
His hands are warm. His heart still beats for me.
The window is foggy, my breath making it so as I look at Him looking at me.

My mother died. I was hurt, lonely.

Surely,
He has not forgotten me but I have forgotten Him, my best friend.
I will go back inside now for I cannot forget the only love I ever knew.

Love Enough

How I long to climb inside the hollow caves of sadness
in your eyes and weep with you the tears that must be wept.
And if I could, you know I would
love you in the way you need to be loved.
But even then would the cavern of pain
be filled or only silenced for a while?

There is a man who knows and understands the fears
that call your name.
He hears what no one sees and sees what you alone hear
in the midnight hours when shadows fall and you feel the
need to quietly slip away.
Once this man hung on a lonely cross
thinking of the day that you would call His name.
And all the while seeing you smile when you
finally understood His love.
He waits for you with love enough to climb inside
your pain and weep with you the tears He's already tasted.

And on that day, I promise to hold a candle for you, my friend,
giving you enough light to see the fire of healing love in His eyes.

Regret

I am sorry my love, so sorry.
The ground is cold.
Snow is falling on your grave.
My heart so warm, bleeding with regret.

I am so sorry!

Please my God, forgive my faithless heart
that was afraid to trust.
Afraid to do the right thing.
To proud to seek Your face for wisdom.

I am so sorry, my love!
Sorry for the words I didn't say.
For the love I never expressed when you were here
with me on this side of the grave.
Foolish was I to think that you would always be there
while I played in forbidden fields.

If I had just one more chance I'd do it differently.
I'd speak the words you needed to hear.
I'd wait for God's best.

Can you forgive me, my love?
God, can you?

"If we confess our sins God is faithful and
just and will forgive us our sins and
cleanse us from all unrighteousness."

I John 1:9

photo by Alyssa Tanner

Little Boy Missing

He's gone, the papers say.
They've given up looking for him.
But I cannot stop looking for him!
How could I?
When I still see him playing in the backyard by
The swing set with dirt all over his face and a pocketful of worms.
When I still hear him calling me,
'"Mama, come look! See what I can do!"

I still feel his soft cheek on my lips when I kissed him
Good night all clean and sweet smelling
Waiting for his bedtime story, Teddy tucked up
With him under the covers.

He's not gone.
Never will he be gone.
Forever my sweet boy,
Forever you will be in your mama's heart.

photo by Rebecca Grant

Lorene Masters

One

I am no longer one of two appearing as one to the world.
But I am only one broken apart from two.
Alone.
Again.
I loved you from the beginning and still do now at the end.

Why? Why did you choose another?
Why did you break the vows we made before God and man?
Love on if you must, my love
While my heart breaks
for our love, that will never be again.
Love on without me.
But I can never love another for you have taken my heart
and thrown it to the dogs.
They are fighting over it now and
it hurts!
Soon the wind shall blow the uneaten pieces away
to a lonely desert where no life can exist.

How will I ever put my heart back together again?

*"God is near to the brokenhearted and saves
those who are crushed in spirit."*

Psalm 34:18

photo by Christina Fuhr

For My Daughter

Voices all around me.
Yet, I only hear yours.
Only the sound of your voice
Could make my heart want to live again.

So many voices!
So much noise!
So much pain.
Never-ending pain
And tears, never drying tears.
Oh my sweet daughter!

Why? Why her God when she was so needed here?
Her children cry, Lord.
Can you not hear them when they
Cry alone at night for Mama?
Why did she have to die when so many twice her age live on,
Never acknowledging Your name?
She loved you, Lord.
She loved her husband, her children.

She loved me.
And now I am alone with all these voices.
Please speak above the noise, Lord.
Speak and tell me why?

"He shall cover you with his feathers and
under his wings you shall take refuge."

Psalm 91:4

photo by Lorene Masters

Lorene Masters

The Tin Trailer

He has chosen his trailer as his coffin.
Never letting anyone in, never going out
except for drinks at the bar.
Bringing smoke and a case home to an empty tin trailer
old when he bought it. Older still now
as only love can make a lonely dwelling new.

He has chosen to hurry in, in drunken stupor
quickly shutting the door on all those who
could love him—cursing their memory.
Tight fists form and hit the thin walls of his tin grave.
Dirty mirrors hang in dusty, wallpaper peeling rooms,
cracked from rage and lonesome age.

The doctor at the vets' clinic burned the cancer off his face,
while the cancer in his heart grew blacker still, locking him
in the past, nursing as a lover the ever-full, ever-empty bottle.

Ashtrays overflow as black fingernails claw the itch of hateful
scars reflected in open windows. Hastily blinds are pulled on his cold, emaciated heart,
knocking weeks' worth of uneaten Meals on Wheels
to the floor while his body starves and swelters in ninety plus degrees of noisy, artificial heat.

The blankets on his legs are piled high with cracker crumbs and
hefty worded books that cannot reach and warm the soul
that is unwilling to forgive.

Reading but never learning. Listening but never hearing.

Clinging to imaginary remote controls, prisoner chained to never-changing self, blaming the world for things he himself
has done.

He has chosen his trailer as his coffin
And I cannot get in.

Photo by Dave Masters

Isabel

For Connie

My sweet Izzy-living doll from Heaven.
Please do not break when you cry.
So fragile. So tiny and alone in the glass cradle
With tubes running here and there.
Oh my little Isabel, please grow strong and let me hold you,
Free of illness. Free of infection. Free of pain.
If I could I would trade places with you in a moment.
Do you know how much I love you?

I do not blame God for He has given me a sweet baby bird with a broken wing to nurse,
to love to life, and I have said yes!
As I said yes to your brother and your sister.
They wait to see you—three from one.

No my sweet, do not weep.
I know the pain is great.

I did not want to stop the doctors and the machines that kept your heart beating, keeping you here with me.
Can you understand that I will never forget how our hearts beat together as one
for a while and how mine has never stopped beating for you?

I did not wish to release the pink and white balloons celebrating your short life
on earth but as we laid your body to rest in the little white casket,
I heard you say, "Mommy, that is not me. I am with Jesus."
Oh my sweet, where have you gone?
Your pure, white heart has separated from this world
And flown back to Heaven.
I look up with joy waiting the day we will be together again.
My sweet Isabel.

photo by Brad VonBergen
Lorene Masters

It's Over

For too long I have loved you.
Too long waiting for you to
Give me what I need.
With tears, I must say goodbye
For you cannot save me.

Adam could not save Eve.
Together they were banished from the garden.
Adam guided Eve away from Paradise with heavy heart and regret,
Unable to stop the flow of tears that rolled down Eve's face.
The heart was no longer young.
Love now grew old and angry.
Sin had come to reign
And shouted in illness and murder and great sobs of agony
When Eve breathed her last.
Adam, unable to stop the wrinkles of time,
Kissed Eve goodbye and cursed the curse of fallen man.

Likewise, as Adam, you cannot save me.
You cannot fill the empty hole.
Oh, I have tried to make you my lord.
I have worshipped you.
Yet the hole remained.

Yes, I love you and know you love me, but my heart still searches
For the One who loved me first.
Loved me best.
I will return to the garden in search of Him.
He still calls my name. Can you hear Him?
For He calls for you, too.
In every breeze, He's there.
In every bird song,
In every waterfall.

For too long He has loved me.
Waiting to give me what I need.
And at last, finally, I have said,
"Yes, Lord, here I am."

photo by Dave Masters

Springtime in Heaven

When this world's winter has known its last,
My heart will long to know,
The greening of the flowers and fields
In Heaven's springtime show.

For the winter has been long and hard
And we've grown weak from cold and fears.
We long for Jesus to say, "Come!
Let me heal your heart and dry all your tears."

For He too has known the darkness of winter,
His bones have felt its deathly chill.
He knows how the spirit grows weary
In waiting for prophecy to be fulfilled.

Soon the Father shall beckon Him
To go and get His own,
The ones who cry and wait for freedom
From winter's dark and dreary home.

He knows that we are longing,
For the hour has long grown late,
Waiting for the newness of body and soul
As we pass through Heaven's eternal gate.

Springtime in Heaven we shall know,
When we lay down our shield and sword,
Having fought the fight and finished the race,
And now He shall be our reward.

Who Knows?

Who knows how winter changes to spring.
Cold and dark one day,
Warm and sunny the next.
Who knows how a heart begins to heal.
Bleeding and broken one day
Mending and hopeful the next.

Who knows how He comes and binds up our wounds
Loving our brokenness into new life.
Who know when?
Who knows how?

We don't need to know but simply trust
That as sure as spring follows winter
There is a time for everything.
A time to be born and a time to die.
A time to weep and time to laugh.
A time to mourn and a time to dance.

The darkness is not forever.
Weeping shall cease.
Joy will come.
Winter will turn to spring.
Wait and see.
For He knows.

"For if we hope for what we do not see,
then we eagerly wait for it with perseverance."

Romans 8:25

photo by Dave Masters

Our God

Our God is not a God who
forsakes us when we are weak.
But rather comes along
beside us to strengthen us.

He is not a God who hurries
past hospital rooms
afraid to come near.
But one who walks the halls
at the painful midnight hours listening
for the invitation to enter in.
Always coming when invited,
pulling up a chair alongside a bed,
holding a hand, wiping a tear—
staying when others leave.

And though He could wipe away
all pain and suffering in a moment,
He waits for us to choose Him
for who He is and not just for what He can do.

Our God is not a God who
forsakes us when we are weak.
But through the suffering He has known
calls us to His side, showing us Himself;
through the weakness of the baby in the manger,
The agony of the man upon the cross and the coming resurrection of all who know Him.

For in spite of sorrow, in spite of pain,_
in spite of the unanswered questions.
He is true and strong,
the power of His resurrection sure!
One day making all wrongs right
and giving eternal joy, peace, and life to all
who seek His strength in their weakness today.

photo by Dave Masters

On Envy

Lord, you see her.
You know that she has flown much higher than I
And stayed up much longer.

Her colors have been more brilliant than mine,
and more have come to see her in flight while I have been
grounded against my will.

She has known lasting
applause it seems, and esteem
from man while I have been
hidden in shadows,

God, forgive my jealous heart
that compares and cannot
rest when I see the wing-span
of one more visible than I.

Forgive my discontent
that refuses to look to
You for worth in the
whirlwind of earthly flight.
In error seeking the passing
pleasure of man's approval
never there for long,
never sure.

Help me to keep my eyes on You—
My heart with You.
Cause me to cease drifting
into lands and emotions
that could harm me.
I long to soar high with You,
wanting only Your approval.
Change me, Lord.
Teach me to fly
for Your eyes only.

Please Hear Me

She awakes.
Just when she hoped she'd sleep forever.
Crying like a baby wanting to be fed.
Where is her daddy?
Where is her momma?
She's all alone, you know.
All alone like an orphan.

Father, please hear me.
You're all I have.
Father, please heal me.
You're all that can.

She sleeps.
Just when she thought she'd be awake forever.
Crying like a baby wanting to be fed.
Where is her daddy?
Where is her momma?
She's all alone, you know.
All alone like an orphan.

"I will not leave you orphans. I will come to you."
John 14:18

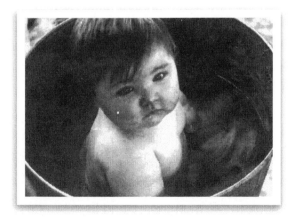

photo by Ron Meland

I Find You in Poetry

I find you in poetry
for I can have you no other way.
Rain drops pelting the fabric of my heart;
caressing soft cotton on cool October nights.

Cold cat meowing to be let in
to the warmth of your presence;
hot soup waiting on the stove.

Warm me, Poetry.
Feed me, for I am hungry and
alone sitting at my kitchen table.

Know him, Poetry, as I do.
For eternal love is strong and longs
to burst forth from behind gray skies.

Paint my kitchen yellow, Poetry.
Yellow as the sun that hasn't
come to visit for awhile.

Love him, Poetry, for I cannot
though I do alone in my kitchen.
Just me with the soup boiling over
and the cat clinging to the screen door
in hopes that I will notice that winter has come.

Find him, Poetry, before the cold
draft drifts under the door and
chills my heart in death.

Find him for me.

"To everything there
is a season, a time
for every purpose under
Heaven. A time to love..."

Ecclesiastes 3:1, 8

photo by Alyssa Tanner

My Sister is Gone

Oh, my sister, you're gone! Even, when we fought growing up
And I wished you away from me
I never wanted this.

Even when you stole my boyfriend and
Told me I was fat and
I scratched your arms with my hairbrush
I never wanted you dead.

Now who can I remember with?
Remember Mom and crazy Dad
Yelling 'til the neighbors called the cops.

Remembering together of playing in the garage
And catching lizards in the cellar
And making mud pies in the summer.

Who will remember with me
The love that came late and lingered long
And past affections that quickly tantalized
And left early?

Who will laugh with me at the memories that
Only we share?
Of Saturday mornings eating cold cereal and frozen
Crème pies, watching cartoons waiting for Mom
To come home from the cafe?

Of track meets where we both got dead last
Yet hugged each other like we were
Olympian gold medallists.

Oh, my sister,
How could you go and die
When there are so many more memories
To make and remember?

photo by Dave Masters

I Love You

I did not choose to love you.
It happened one day in a moment of time.
I had no control, no choice,
I knew and loved you so deeply, so eternal.
Caring so much that your every pain broke my heart.

I love loving you.
Though it is so lonely.
Though I go about my days
With empty arms.
For God said no, not now.
Wait and trust.

Someday will my heart be satisfied?
Will I feel your heart beating with mine,
Racing towards eternity?
How the longing hurts today!
Like the constant pricking of a rose thorn
Of which I cannot get free,
I hurt and hurt and hurt.

Yet the sweet scent of tomorrow is there
For I have chosen to wait for
The you I have never touched.
And the you who has never touched me.

I love you.

Farewell

I have known you
When shadows from silent meadows fell
Imprisoning bleeding memories around your heart.
I loved you when your pain was great and you suffered alone.
In my heart, I have held you as the grief escaped.

I have prayed abundant life for you,
Sensing the beauty of freedom's cry.
Knowing you'd be strong one day.

Farewell to the silent meadow of memories.
Go now and grow,
Be what you were always meant to be.
And know that you do not walk alone.

"Those who sow in tears shall reap in joy."
Psalm 127:5

Photo by Rachel Masters

When I See You

When I see you looking at me,
Your long, blond hair blowing in the wind,
Your sad forlorn eyes,
Your sometimes smile.
The clothes you wear.
I see rainy days and Bee Gees,
Warm summer nights and yellow pickup trucks
With a cast iron gas pedal in the shape of a foot.
Blue cars and icy roads and snow piled high everywhere
Dancing in a white dress, dreams coming true that I never thought would.

You didn't know your kindness would change my world, give me hope.
You didn't know that I could not help falling in love with you.
You never took advantage of me.
Only tried to love me because I loved you and my heart was so lonely.

Please know that in the old me and the new me, a part of me will always love you.
I want you to know that in case you sometimes feel that no one loves you
Or accepts you.
I never tried to change you.
I was only scared for you and me.
I don't want to go back but I do wish that we could love each other now.
Wind of change blew.
The barrier between us is too big. We may never end up together.
Still, I think you are beautiful.
I have learned to make it alone.
But sometimes I cry,
For you.

Photo by Irene Meland

Please Love Me

It's that time of year again when the land becomes
dark too soon and cold icicles form
hanging lonely, long and slim from my window.
Birds have left their playground in the sky
and flown to a new place of sunshine and hope.

Alone at night I felt the chill of days and friends gone by.
Its eeriness becomes me as I cried for you to remember me
and to please love me.

"No longer will they call you deserted or name your
land Desolate, for the Lord will take delight in you"

Isaiah 62:4

photo by Jamie Knapp

Autumn Love

Love you, I do.
When the first leaves of autumn
Fell down around my feet
Chasing the summer heat
From my heart into the cold
Realities of today.
For it is not my right to dream of
Holding you this season
Yet I cannot help to dream of springtime.
Even if I dream alone.
Oh, the beauty of your life.
The gift from God that you are.
My hopes are in the seasons of tomorrow for my heart
Knows not the time of year to stop loving you.

I can see eternity in your eyes.
I see love always from the beginning to the end.
Wait, my love, for our season shall come.
Wait.
I see the summer sun shining on autumn leaves
Spring flowers floating in the fresh stream of melted snow.
The hope of all our winter longing fulfilled at last.
In a moment of time.
Wait.
I shall come.

"I waited patiently for the Lord; and
he inclined unto me and heard my cry."

Psalm 40:1

photo by Rachel Masters

Healing Love

I shiver in the warmth of your love
As winter calls me away
To your waiting arms.
My lips are chilled upon yours.
Why must she live within your eyes
When our hearts meet?
Why can't you leave her
Where she left you?
Alone.
I love you!
The call of spring has come.
Listen! Hear the sweet songs of melody within my heart
Singing of love,
Healing love forever and ever.

photo by Rachel Masters

If Only

If only you could see with me
Like we used to see when we were together.
Maybe then, we wouldn't have to be apart now.

If only you could love me
Like you used to love me when our love
Was new and hope lived in your eyes.

If only you could see how
My love has not changed only been rearranged
To try and fit into your world.

If only you could see with me
Like we used to see when we were together.
Maybe then, we could be together now.

Thy Will Be Done

Oh Lord, please don't let out
Future loving live alone in the flower
Of forgotten passion, summers ending
Never to be known in this world.

Don't let our longing find us
Empty, wilted bodies, weary heart
Aching for what could have been.

And please don't let our affections
Tearful fall on a cold tombstone
In a lonely graveyard
Praying still for our hearts to beat
As one eternal in You.

But Lord,
If tears must fall,
If sadness must be known
Then Love, heal us.
Love hold us.
Love fill us.

Thy will be done!

Photo by Tina Weiss

Lorene Masters

Power

I know His power
In the tempest sea where
Hearts are tossed to and fro and
Fear lives in the depths of
Ocean blue memories.

I feel His power in the quiet
Stillness of a spring morning where
Dew rests at home on green blades
Of new grass.

I spoke of possible rejection and the
Seas whose winds could break
The windows of my heart.

You spoke of the hope of healing
The beautiful view of springtime
Through the broken windows of
Yesterday's winters.

Hearts of glass know His strength
Of steel, and the raging sea is not
Surprised when His voice whispers
"Peace, peace be still."

Photo by Brendon Fuhr

Hands

God, why does the little happiness I hunger for
Have such a high price tag? Why does it never seem to be on sale?

My heart is not for sale.
To be picked over, played with and then
Discarded and labeled "damaged in transit."

Why do my desires cost so much of me,
Bring me so much pain in life's checkout line?

Waiting forever but always coming up short,
Hands, dirty hands, cruel hands
Grabbing, grabbing, grabbing at me
Stop!
Please stop.
Stop asking for more than I can give.
More than I've ever had.
My pocketbook is empty still with
No one near to pay the price.

Lord, I know, I've shopped in every heart but Yours.
Taken every hand but Yours.
Forgive me, but I never understood the scars You carry.
Yet, I wonder—could Your scarred hands heal my scarred heart?

"And when he had spoken to them,
He showed them His hands."

Luke 24:40

photo by Alyssa Tanner

Lorene Masters

35

I Know the Reason

I know the feeling of coming home into a warm room
From an icy cold winter's night in which I wore a
Dress and thin stockings.
The itch as feet come alive again
Feeling the warmth of the carpet.

I know the meaning of grief so overwhelming that it seems as
Though you too have died while your body is forced to stay
And breathe and breathe day after endless year.

I know the reason why He came.
Because I hurt and you hurt.
We are cold. He is warmth.
We are dead. He is life eternal.
Life far beyond the hardest hurt on the coldest day that
You spend alone remembering.

If it is Real

If it is real
It will not fade quietly into the sunset
Never to be seen again.
If it is real it will rise with the morning sun.
It will shine brighter and brighter until it finds a home.
If it is real.

illustration by Hannah Masters

The Tin Trailer and other Poems for the Hurting and the Hopeful

It's Coming

The darkness comes slowly
Soaring on a familiar hurt from the past.
You know it's coming yet
You run around with flashlights
And torches trying to keep the day burning bright.
Trying to keep the happy feelings as long as you can.

But the inevitable valley of the shadow of death comes.
Flooding your world
Plunging your heart and mind into darkness that
No human light could ever touch.

"The darkness and the light are
both alike to You"

Psalm 139:12

In Your Eyes

I look into your eyes
And I can feel the pain they've known.
The dull darkness of them I see
As they become translucent
In the bright sun of today.

It hurts to see you this way.
Knowing that your laughter is a mask to all your sorrow.
Knowing that my heart
Will still be here for you tomorrow
On the sidewalk by the house
With all the purple flowers
Where you kissed me and said goodbye.

Now you are somewhere else away from me.
Your pain in full bloom.
The sleepless nights and endless days.
I remember you and think of you always.

photo by Alyssa Tanner

Photo by Alyssa Tanner

The Passage of Life

He lay there as if asleep.
His days on earth
Were a short lifetime.

And friends and relatives came
To cry and remember
The days spent together.

As you look upon his face and see the eyes
Whose blue will never shine again,
Memories come flooding back
Causing you to feel as though you
Will drown in your pain.

More than anything you yearn for the past
Which can never come again except
In the mind's playground.
You long for just one more yesterday
To bid your farewell.

But no ...
His train came, which only boarded him
In the early morning hours of his life.

A couple of miles down the track stood
Everyone who loved him.
And like a seagull without a sea
To soar above they remained.
Why?
Tell me why?
And later, what now?
He's gone.
And it feels like little solace to say
"He's gone to a much better place"
when you must remain here without him.

Yet, somehow,
The human survival instinct prevails
And you live one.
Slowly, going on, remembering and never forgetting
How precious life is and realizing how much
You really loved someone.

photo by Alyssa Tanner

Wait for Me

Wait for me,
For I am old and the troubles of my heart
Have enlarged.

Wait for me,
For my bones are tired
And movement makes them ache.

Wait for me,
And if you get to the top of the hill
Before I do turn around and see if I
Am following still.

If you see that I have fallen,
Please come back and help me up and
Wait for me to take that first step again
As I once waited for you to take yours
And learn to tie your shoes
Or stop to examine a bug on the sidewalk
Or finish your homework or come home late at night.

Wait for me until the end,
Which shall come quickly now.
For I am old and the troubles of my heart have enlarged.

"Cast your cares on the Lord and He shall sustain you"

Psalm 55:22

Photo by Dave Masters

Lorene Masters

The Race for Life

The gun sounded. The race began.
You left the starting blocks of your yesteryears behind.

At times you unwisely paced the way
Which caused you to prematurely tire on some long home stretches.

But at other times you moved in such a way that your opponents
Simply stepped aside and let you pass.
With each corner that you rounded, you grew and loved and laughed and cried.

You weren't ever alone, for someone was always there watching
And cheering you on to the finish.

Even when the sky cried
And the world was chilled
And your usually loyal fans fled to the security of their homes, He stayed.
Because of the rain and the pain that filled your eyes you couldn't always see Him.
But He was there on the top bleachers with an overcoat and umbrella in hand watching you and hoping that you'd
glance up and catch the love in His eyes.
Every race he came and all of Heaven rejoiced the day you accepted
His Life Everlasting Award.

*"I will be a father to you and you
will be my sons and daughters."*

2 Corinthians 6:18

Bread of Life

Oh, Bread of Life
A sparrow has fallen
Did you see?
I saw it when I came down the stairs.
Landed right at my feet and
Tried to fly.
I wanted to help him find the courage
For flight but his pain was too great.

Oh, Bread of Life,
A lamb is lost.
She wandered away last night during
A blinding storm of heart and mind.
Thought she knew the way but night
Came, black as sin
And she fell.
Did you see?

Oh, Bread of Life,
My wings are broken and I am lost
In the vast darkness.
After eating my fill of wandering,
I hunger.
After drinking of the night,
I thirst.
Bread of Life,
Find me, fill me, heal me.

The Butterflies Have Gone

The butterflies have gone.
No more colors waving on
Flimsy flower petals
On hot summer days.

No more fluttering wings
Arriving unexpectedly
On picnics or walks.

No more.
Until next year.

But God
Has made a way for
Life to live on in the shadow
Of season's end.

For He is life,
He is color.
He is beauty everlasting.

The butterflies have gone.
But He lives on forever
In the summer of our memories.

photo by Rachel Masters

I Love You, Momma

Momma, I love you more than I can say.
I know that I am young, yet I
Feel your pain of the years.
I know why you cry.
I understand your tears.
Momma, I long to give you hope and a
Constant stream of love.
So often I feel I love you more than anyone.
With every rising sun you will always be the only
Mother God gave to me.
Please always remember whether I am near or far that it's you mother,
Whom I hold so dear.

I miss you in times when hours somehow climb into years.
Realizing that this life is but a breath and soon, so soon we'll be with Jesus living in His depth.
Remembering no more the pain of hard cutting rains and days spent lonely and alone,
Missing children no longer home.
Soon, so soon, we'll no longer roam but be with Jesus in His heavenly home.

Joanna in Worship

Hands, beautiful hands
Long and slender,
Lily-white fingers open, holding one
Heart reaching upward,
Touching Him who gave.
Embraced by love, knowing life
Abundant life in Him.

Hands. Bleeding hands,
Long and slender.
Crimson-rose fingers broken as one
Heart reaching downward.
Touching us who bleed.
Embracing with love, giving life,
Abundant life in Him.

Hands, beautiful hands,
Long and slender,
Lily-white fingers open, holding one
Heart reaching downward,
Touching us who hurt.
Embracing in love, praying life,
Abundant life in Him.

Storming the Gates of Hell

Leaving the sunshine to storm the gates of Hell.
Looking for a sign of you.
Conversations past haunt me.
I fear for your soul.
Taking hold of prayer, I run.
Passing many on the way I
Run until I can see your face.
So easily you let your mind slip away to that dark and lonely place.
So easy for you to think that this is where you will find freedom.
Not realizing that your quest for freedom could put others in chains
That are not easily broken.

I am so sorry for your pain, for your loneliness, for your sadness.
I know that it is not quickly solved with a word or a pill.

I find you like a crippled, old man all snarled up and bent
With fear, lying alone in the darkness, empty pill bottle nearby.
I search for your hand, carefully unfolding the fingers that
Hold your hopes and hurts.
Sitting beside you, I wait.
Feeling your pain with you in the quiet as
Tears finally fall.
Isolation broken as you let me in.
You are not alone.
You are loved.

How could this of happened!
Why did you not call?
Why did you not reach out like all the times before when the pain
Was great in your heart and mind?
Did you not know that I would always be there for you?
What could I have done differently? Why did I not see?

I lift your head to my breast and weep.
With you.
Heart so raw and bleeding

Rising I carry you to Him.
He will receive you.
He will wipe away every tear from your eyes.

He will heal the part that I could not.
The part the doctors could not understand.
As the ambulance speeds away, red lights blaring
I release you to
The One who died to set you free.
The One who took the keys of Hell and
The grave so you could live
Whole in the sunshine of His love.
Forever

"The Law of the Spirit of life in Christ Jesus has made me free from the law of sin and death."

Romans 8:2

photo by Alyssa Tanner

The Stroke

Today I tried to talk to you but I could not.
I tried to squeeze your hand but my hands remained
Taut and lifeless.
In my heart I held you
And loved you as much as always even though my voice
Could not be heard.
I long to speak!
I want to tell you that you look lovely
In that new shirt—after all, blue is your best color.
And that I am sick to death of oatmeal.
And that the extra paper towels are in the
Basement under the sheets where I put them
Before this all happened.
Before I fell and everything changed.

Today I tried to tell you that I can still see with my heart.
I still see you so clearly.
And I can hear!
I want to tell you that I can hear your every word.
And I can feel your hand on mine.
I need to feel your hand on mine.
I am cold.
I hate being imprisoned in this body.

Please speak to me not as an invalid but
As your mother.
That has not changed. I am still your mother.
Though I cannot speak.
Cannot see too well. Cannot feed myself.
Cannot move
I can still love.
Always I will love.

"So fix your eyes not on what
is seen but what is unseen. For
what is seen is temporary but
what is unseen is eternal."

2 Corinthians 4:18

photo by Lorene Masters

Lorene Masters

49

The Car Accident

Why?
Why did my Anna have to be on that street at that time of day when
That drunk driver was out?

Where were you protecting angels, Lord?
Why could they not be there when my Anna needed them?

She was only going to run to the store to get some
Milk and bread for the kids' breakfasts.

She was going to be home in thirty minutes
In time to get dinner ready, and help the kids with their
Homework and get them ready for tomorrow.
Only thirty minutes, Lord!
Were You off duty for the thirty minutes my Anna was out?
She was all I had.
My beautiful wife, my childhood sweetheart.
And now she is gone.
She died instantly the police officer said.
And I died too at that exact moment.

How do I tell the kids that their mama is not coming home
Ever again? How?

Oh God, why
Did Your Son have to die?
Why is there so much pain and sorrow in this world?
Why?

photo by Lorene Masters

"And God will wipe away every tear from their
eyes; there shall be no more death, nor sorrow,
nor crying, and there shall be no more pain,
for the former things have passed away."

Revelation 21:4

The Tin Trailer and other Poems for the Hurting and the Hopeful

Baby Mandy

Just tissue, they said, not viable.
Simple procedure, just a few hours and it's all over.
Problem gone.
No one needs to know.

But I know and so does Kay.
The bleeding from my body slowed
And stopped as they said it would.
But my heart bleeds on.

Did my baby have a heartbeat?
Did she hurt when it stopped?
Who would she have looked like?
Would she have had Paul's big blue eyes and my smile?
Would she have liked to sing and play softball?
I watch the fifth graders get off the bus and wonder
Would she have run home like them wanting a snack and a hug?

Curling up on the couch in the fetal position, tissues pressed to my face,
I weep with regret for what will never be.
I could have given her life.
I could have given her to someone who couldn't have kids.

My parents never knew.
We were so young.
Our whole lives before us, the counselor said.
It was better for everyone this way.
Simple procedure.
Not!
It was not and will never be a
Simple procedure.

I released a pink balloon for her today.
I watched it until it was no more.
Swallowed up in the fluffy white clouds.
A pink balloon for my baby Mandy.
She'd be ten today.
Oh, I love you, my baby!
I am so sorry I did not let you live.
Wait for me, Mandy.
Wait, Mama's coming.

"The Lord is near to those who have a broken heart."

Psalm 34:18

Lorene Masters

The Death of a Career

Stuffed Shirt came
And told me to pack up my office.
It's been long enough and I haven't
Delivered enough of the goods that this
Company needs to grow.

Huh?

I recall all the hours I spent
After hours making money for the
Company and he tells me I haven't done enough?

The keys in my pocket are heavy
As my heart as I place them on my desk
What will I tell Sharon?
There goes the retirement we were to enjoy
In the sun with the grandkids and leisure
Hours playing golf are gone out the window like a fly that
Buzzes too much and has to go.

Just doing my job, the Stuffed Shirt says.
So sorry but someone has to go.
I got the orders from the Big Guy.
It's you or me. And he laughed.
A sick, sorry sort of laugh that would haunt me
As I sent the résumés out and hit the streets trying to
Gain what I lost in self-respect, hoping they'd not notice that
My hair was gray and turning whiter with each interview I took
Hearing, "We'll let you know,"
Yet never hearing from them again.

Stuffed Shirt died today.
Heart attack.
I won't cry at his funeral
I'm too busy crying at mine.

"For I know the plans I have for you says
the Lord plans for peace and not for
evil to give you a future and a hope."

Roman's 8:28

Living with Lyme

Dumb doctors not knowing what to do
With me and the strange
Rash on my arm even after
I told them that I saw the same
Rash online on someone else's body.
And something did bite me and
No, no, no it's not Lyme Disease.
Silly girl.

Doctors again when I cannot walk
And joints are burning,
Bell's Palsy returning,
Head is pounding,
Words are slurring.
Memory forgotten and
Please, please, please,
Can you tell me
What is wrong with me?

We do not know. Blood does not show
Any problems. Take these and hopefully
You will feel better soon. If not
Come back and we will see what else we can do.

Oh my God, help me!
Do not forsake me.
Man is small and does not know
As much as he thinks he does.
You are great and know all things.

Heal me and I shall be healed.
Save me and I shall be saved.

Dad Doesn't Live Here Anymore

Last night I heard Mama cry after
Dad yelled and now I am scared and
Feel very small in my large bed that I
Wanted so much when I was seven.

Goldie is here. She licks my face as tears
Begin to fall on memories of
The trip we took to Disneyland.
And the boat ride on the lake and the
Happiness I felt when Dad saw me hit my first home run and
Now I can't sleep 'cuz I hear them fighting
Again and I know that he is packing his bags
And going to a place that I cannot go.

Packing for a trip that only
He can take, away from us and me and
With... what did Mom call her? The Project
That Dad always had to work late on?
The Project worked her way into Dad's heart and now
Mine is cold and afraid.

I want to get up and tell Mom that it's okay.
That I will never leave her.
But I know I will.

God please help us!

photo by Alyssa Tanner

Dog Gone

Happy greeting.
Tail wagging.
Love meeting me
At the end of a long, stressful day
Filled with problems and pains
Losses and gains and
Oh, how I love my dog!

Sad parting
Tail stopped
Love going down
To the bottom of a long, deep hole
Filled with dirt and tears
Agony and fears and
Oh, how I loved my dog!

artwork by Hannah Masters

Finding Hannah

One, two, three, twenty, two hundred
Ready or not here I come!
Hannah?
Oh, Hannah, where are you Hannah?

Giggling heard from under the table.
Here I am, Mommy! Jumping out and
Scaring me half to death but mostly laughter
Erupted until Hannah grew and
The hiding became more complicated.

One, two, three, twenty, two hundred
Ready or not here I come!
Hannah? Oh Hannah? Where are you?
Hannah?
No giggles gave her away at first but then
They would start and I would ask,
Am I getting warmer? Did you go outside
And hide in the doghouse? I know, you must be in the cookie jar
Eating all the cookies, Yum! Yum! I love cookies!
And I would open the cookie jar and start to munch
While my heart was slowly being eaten away as
Hannah grew up and away and began to hide in places
That I could not go.

Some days I was too tired to play and wanted things to
Slow down and not change. I wanted Hannah to be where I could always
See her. But the game went on as it had from the beginning
Of mothers and fathers and children who begged to play.
Just one more time Mommy, please.
Okay, just a short game then I have to cook dinner.

One, two, I began.
Oh, I better start the potatoes.
Three, four ...
Do we have any sour cream left?
Five, six
What time is it getting to be?
Seven
Let's see where is that chicken recipe?
Eight
Oven set to 350.

Nine, ten
Why am I counting?

Oh yes, Hannah. Hannah ready or not here I come!
Hannah?
Oh, Hannah, where are you Hannah?
Where are you, Hannah?!

Mom, I'm right here. Why are you yelling?
Uh, dinner is almost ready.
I can't tonight. Have to be at the college by five.
Eleven, twelve, eighteen.
What did you say Mom?
Uh, did you get all packed up?
Yes, I have to go. Goodbye.
Door open, shut.
Goodbye.
Nineteen, twenty.
And who is this "Mom" person? My name is Mommy.
Timer set to rest up on the couch ready for the next game
Of Hide and Go Seek.

Time goes too fast.

photo by Lorene Masters

Soft Padded Paws

For Sabrina the Cat

Soft padded paws meet me at the door
When I return on a cold winter's night
Feeling lonely and alone.

Meowing a greeting that did not stop
Even when it was time for bed.
Jumping in with me under the covers
Being a friend to the friendless.

I think you know, Sabrina.
I think you know when I need you
To be there. To be a soft furry weight
Next to me. I treat you like a kid
And maybe that is why you cry when I leave
And purr for joy when I return.
That is why you want to eat when I eat
And watch TV when I do.

Did you wonder when the household grew and
The man I married came to live with us and
You bit his hand when he touched me?
I had to laugh.
But I was not laughing when the babies came and
My mind was fuzzy and hands too busy to hold you.
I loved you the same. It's just that I loved them more.

I'll always regret the day I had to give you away.

I miss you still, now that the kids are grown and
I am lonely and alone, remembering the
Soft padded paws that would meet me at the door
When I returned on cold winter nights.

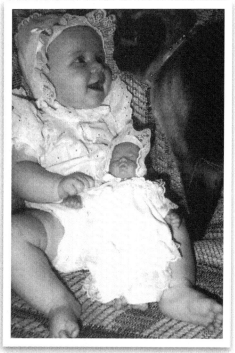

photo by Lorene Masters

Too Deep for Tears

Pain too deep for words.
Sorrow too deep for tears.
I sit alone in the dark
Too weary to get up and turn a light on.
Why should I? When my soul would still be
Dark and afraid and in
Pain too deep for words.
Sorrow too deep for tears.

The Silence of God

From Psalm 22, 143

My God, my God, why have You forsaken me?
Why are You so far from helping me?
I cry in the daytime and You do not hear.
And in the night season I am not silent.
But I am a worm and no man.
Despised of man and rejected of the people.

All who see me laugh me to scorn.
They shoot out the lip saying,
She trusted in God let Him deliver her.
Let Him rescue her since she trusts in Him.

You are He who brought me out of my mother's womb.
You made me trust when I was on my mother's breasts.
Be not far from me for trouble is near and
There is none to help.

For the enemy has persecuted my soul
He has crushed my life to the ground
He has made me dwell in darkness
Like those who have long been dead.
Therefore my spirit is overwhelmed within me
My heart within me is distressed.

Answer me speedily, O Lord;
My spirit fails!
Do not hide Your face from me lest I be like those
Who go down to the pit.

Cause me to hear Your loving kindness in the morning
For in You do I trust.
Revive me, O Lord , for Your name's sake!
For Your righteousness sake, bring my soul out of prison.

photo by Dave Masters

The Tin Trailer and other Poems for the Hurting and the Hopeful

Thoughts Too Full

My thoughts are too full of
You and me together
Loving life with children
That look like you and
Sound like many waters of joy-filled hours
Knowing each other in completeness
That could never be reached alone.

Thoughts too full because my heart
Is completely alone today yet
I dream of you and someday
When the world is new and every darkened hope
Becomes light in the presence of Him who
Created the desires of man
I wait.

Leaving You

Some days leaving you is so painful when I am filled
With a love that cannot be known, cannot be shown
Only felt within my heart when no one else is looking.

The day was cold and cloudy
Yet the warm light dancing in your eyes was so bright,
The music in your voice so clear,
The beauty in your heart so alive with the fragrance of
Spring flowers that can only burst forth after the rain
Has done its labor in the deep darkness of the soil.

I long to feel the tears that hold your sadness.
I long to touch the light in your eyes.
I long to touch you.

Some days missing you is so painful
When I'm filled with a hunger that cannot be known,
Cannot be satisfied only kept alive within my heart,
Praying someday that I will hunger no more.

Faithful Loving

Dedicated to Pastor Curtis Long

Faithful loving since the day we said I do.
Faithful in the old days.
Faithful in the new ways.
Faithful in the dark as in the light
My love was faithful, faithful through and through.

He's been faithful to God since the day he said yes.
Faithful when the going was tough.
Faithful when there was more than enough.
Faithful in the dark as in the light.
As God's child, he was faithful, faithful through and through.

God's been faithful to me since before I was formed.
Faithful when I said no and walked away.
Faithful when I said yes, I'm home to stay.
And like my daddy, He's faithful in the dark as in the light.
My God is faithful, He's faithful through and through.

He's faithful when the way is uncertain
And we don't know what to do.
Faithful when the path is clear
And we're sailing right on through
Faithful in the dark as in the light.
God is faithful, faithful through and through.

One sad day God called my daddy home.
With tears and sorrow we watched him go.
But God received him as His very own and
Said, "Welcome home My son, enter into thy rest
Thou good and faithful servant."

You've been faithful in the hard times,
Faithful in the good,
Faithful in the dark as in the light.
You've been faithful, faithful through and through.

Faithful loving
Beginning to the end
Faithful loving
World without end.

photo by Tommy Quinn

Two Funerals

There were two funerals today.
One for a man of God loved by all.
The other for a modern thief on the cross.

I wish I could say that I attended the funeral for the man of God
That I knew him well: had always known him.
Identified with him and all he was and stood for.
Were good friends with his children, accepted into their circle.

But no, I was not present at his funeral, though my thoughts and prayers
Were there with his precious family and friends,
My body was with the thief on the cross, for he was my father.

Scarce were the guests at his funeral.
A few relatives and drinking buddies.
It was cold and
Rain fell in lonely drops on the kids who came. Chilling them
In heart for what they never had and never will.

God received him into His kingdom, we hoped but could not be sure.
I wonder—did he see the other man receive his welcome or was he ushered away
And seated in a forlorn spot for the lack of accolades he obtained?

Did they speak on how they both knew me?
One a little, one a lot.
Were they equal in heaven?
Or did the shame of his life live on?

If God is like this precious Man of God and this Man of God is like God,
I think that he was loved.
I think that, as God understood the thief on the cross,
He also understood my dad and why he was the way he was and why his kids
Are the way they are and He loves us still.
The unlovely ones, the embarrassment of society,
The ones who try and try to get it right—confessing each time after they fall into sin,
Nursing the bottle because they never had a mama or a daddy or any self-worth at all.
I think that God will make all things fair and right.

I think that what we see in heaven will be so different than what we've known on earth.
There will be a place for all who called upon the name of the Lord.

The unlovely ones, the poor, the weak.
I think that God will heal all wounds and give us another chance—
Those who cried out for salvation again and again.
Those whose sins have killed them as our sins killed Him.

I think God was at both funerals.

Loss of a Friendship

It's come to this then, has it?
You go your way.
I'll go mine.
Stubbornly refusing to see another's point of view.
Wanting only your will and your way to be fulfilled.
Not willing to change and be something new
But blaming your troubles on everyone else
When a simple, "I'm sorry, I blew it,"
Could refresh and renew
Our friendship of many years.

I can only suppose then, that this is God
Setting me free from fetters
And attitudes that bind. Blinding me to His best.
Free of dysfunction
And dependency on another
Other than Him.
I pray someday that you will see the freedom that is there
By forgiving and forgetting
And submitting to the One
Who is greater than yourself.

Project Rescue

Dedicated to Mike and Denise Bartel

There is a darkness that exists behind closed doors.
Young girls being lied to, ripped from their
Childhood, forced to grow up as victims of
Black hearts driven by greed and the need to survive,
Sell them for a pittance, not caring for their soul as they
Rob, kill, and destroy, working the works of the devil.
Girls in pain, cold and afraid thinking no one sees, no one cares.

There is a light that overcomes
As valiant soldiers of the Cross
Go forth to the streets, fighting for the freedom
Of the soul God came to save.
Illuminating the darkness with His presence
Not fearing those who kill the body but cannot
Kill the soul, knowing that there is nothing covered that
Will not be revealed or hidden that will not be known.
Rescuing the helpless.
Trusting the One who is greater
Who sees and hears the cries of those in
Slavery still. Dark dungeon doors
Break open wide when you answer the
Cries of the little ones with no voice, no choice.

He wants to answer through you.

Ricky

They came and took him away today.
My big brother Ricky.

Daddy called them and they came, barging into our world
Wearing long, white jackets and shiny black boots.
Putting him in a straitjacket. Mama holding the spoon
Firm in his mou th so he wouldn't swallow his tongue.
I would wonder how someone could swallow his tongue
For years to come.

He won't hurt you anymore, Daddy said.
What? Hurt us?
My big brother who played with me under the Christmas tree
At midnight on Christmas Eve?
My brother who laughed at everything anyone said?
My brother Ricky who was so like me only bigger?
Hurt us?

I know he didn't mean to smash pop bottles on his head
Down by the railroad tracks.
Or chase Larry and Jerry around the yard with 2 x 4s when he was mad.
And it was an accident when the lawn dart got stuck in my back
And I had to go to the emergency room

Mama's crying, mumbling something about a place called Redfield.
Ricky will never come home again.
He will always be four years old, they said.
And I will always miss him.

photo by Dave Masters

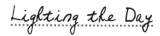

Lighting the Day

How I dread the darkness of morning
When fears awake to whisper
In my ear that God is asleep
And far removed from my troubles.

When feelings rule all reason and
One is paralyzed in thought
And body with what ifs? And whys?
When the sky is black with clouds
Where just yesterday the sun shone so brightly.

Please, Lord, be light!
Be bright, shining light
And pierce my darkness
With Your presence.
For without seeing
I choose to believe
That You are there,
That You are good,
That You care.

My life and times are in Your hands
So why should I fear?

My God, my rock shall keep me safe from all eternal harm.
For in Him is hope
And peace and light,
Bright shining light
In the darkest of days.

photo by Alyssa Tanner

Cup of Cold Water

Some say that the cruelest rain, the coldest, the most wet
Falls where no one sees.
The barren land with an invisible resistance to moisture,
The hard-packed pain of generational hopelessness.
The starving child crying, searching for bread and love
And a place to belong.
Wondering why they must hunger and wander alone
With bloated bellies devoid of nourishment and hope.
Questioning, is there a God? And does He see? Does He care?
Weak little hands holding empty bowls
Fighting off the flies of infection
Trying to survive without mother or father
On violent, uncaring streets of endless misery.

Well, I say the cruelest, the coldest, the most wet
Rain does fall, but He has seen and answered through you
In what you give and what you keep.
In going to them and staying home to pray.
In believing that He is big enough to fill the void
Of those hungry for so much more than food.

You answer the cry of His great heart by
Showing His love to the forgotten.
Knowing that He will not forget the cup of cold water
You gave to the thirsty soul.

Quest for Comfort

I swept up the remnants of my quest for comfort off
The kitchen floor while you looked on mocking me and
My hunger so great, the loneliness so acute since
We quit each other.
Crusty crumbs under the counter. Flakes laced with chocolate,
White flour, dusty
On my lonely broom bristles.
No comfort was found for long
In things that only fill the stomach.

It has become your choice.
Your silence saying more than words ever could.

The Empty Tomb Is Speaking

The empty tomb is speaking
of the life that is to come.
Eternal life full of peace and joy
when our work on earth is done.

No more crying, pain, or death.
All sorrow will be washed away
when Jesus breaks through the clouds
taking His children home to stay.

He's gone to prepare a place for us.
So many are already there.
That great multitude of believers all waiting
for the marriage supper we will share.

Our redemption our Savior has won
through the rugged Cross of Calvary.
Light has overcome the darkness.
The blind at last can see.

The empty tomb is speaking
of promises yet to be known
Look quickly inside for His glory
soon comes for us—His very own.

Photo by Lorene Masters

Country Music Makes Me Cry

Country music makes me cry
When you're not here with me
To catch my tears when they fall
And hold me in your arms--just loving me.

Country music makes me cry
When you're so far away.
And I find myself all alone again
Praying I can find my way.

When the old songs play and Johnnie's
Having a Sunday morning coming down
And Willie's on the road again.
Dolly's wearing that coat of many colors and
A Rhinestone Cowboy's got country boy Glen.

It's then, that country music makes me cry
When you're not here with me
To catch my tears when they fall
And hold me in your arms--just loving me.

Country music makes me cry
When you're so far away.
And I find myself all alone again
Praying I can find my way.

When Josh is on that long black train and
Tim's having a good morning beautiful,
Trace has got his guitar out to aint sing no love song
And Faith is hoping to breath while crying just a little.

When Alan is trying to have a good time I'm not! 'cuz
Country music makes me cry
When you're not here with me
To catch my tears when they fall
And hold me in your arms--just loving me.

Country music makes me cry
When you're so far away.
And I find myself all alone again
Praying I can find my way.

Dancing on Your Grave

Oct 12, 1961-

I saw you so clearly in my dream last night;
Your name and birth date shone in the moon's glow.
Your dance was so charming, so light on your feet as you
Tapped out a rhythm on your tombstone below.

It was like watching a movie that starred only you
As you moved from one girl to the next.
Twirling and swirling while the drink in your hand
Emptied and filled as though touched by a hex.

More kisses, more hugs, more promises
All so sincere at the time they were made.
But never remembered when the sun came up
As you were dancing on your grave.

Look at your feet so young and alive.
Look closely under the fading sun's glow.
Look quickly for time hurries on
And you have only one chance to know

That the music will end, the curve will come fast
Death will stop for you too and not wait.
You're dancing alone now on your grave for
Your time has come; you're at Eternity's gate.

Your dance ends quickly. Your partners are all gone.
The music has stopped.
No more laughter. No more songs.

You're alone, all alone now dancing on your grave.
All alone, all alone.
I see you dancing on your grave.
All alone.

"For what will it profit a man to gain the whole world if he loses his own soul?"
Matthew 16:26

A New Song

Can you hear the Spirit calling?
Calling you to sing a new song?
A song of love and forgiveness
To cover all your wrongs.

A song of hope in sadness
And laughter through your tears.
A song of peace in the storms
And freedom from all your fears.

Come and sing a new song.
He has one that's all your own.
He knows your every longing
He's waiting to welcome you home.

Can you hear the Spirit calling?
Listen closely and you soon will
Hear a voice speaking of love and hope
For the future he has for you still.

Hear the Spirit calling.
Hear His voice today.
Hear the Spirit calling
Come, He's made a way.

Come now.
Hear the Spirit calling
Calling you away.
Come. Come.

Goodbye

Your voice sounded sad on the phone.
I know you are tired of it all.
Tired of the pain, the uncertainty.
I know you love me.
You needn't say a word.
I will stay here awhile on the other end
And feel the sadness with you.

And please know that when all is said and done
That you will not be so easy to forget.
It will not be so simple to bury your memory with
Things that don't matter anymore.
I will still see your eyes. Still feel your heart
Beat with mine and remember when we said
Goodbye for the last time.

Love So Deep

Love so deep hurts.
Hurts deeper still when betrayed.
Isolation.
Fear.
Tears that seem to have no end.
Memories of past rejections
Replay in the darkness.
Sleep will not come.
Is it truly better to have loved and lost
Than never to have loved at all?
I don't think so.
For whoever wrote those words never
Had to live after losing you.

"Greater love has no one than this, than he lay down his life for his friends."
John 15:13

Affair with the World

One smile too many,
One look too long,
One conversation too fulfilling,
One marriage soon gone.

One heart too empty,
One mind too dull,
One life too weary,
One's passions too full,
To even think of staying to try and work it out.
Vows made to Thee are binding
But hope is filled with doubt because of

One smile too many,
One look too long,
One conversation too fulfilling,
One marriage soon gone.

Being married isn't easy
'Cuz the devil's got a plan
But God's plan is far greater
Than we could ever understand.
We're the Bride of Christ
Waiting for our groom.
So let's prepare our hearts
He's coming for us soon.

Let's not have
One smile too many,
One look too long,
One conversation too fulfilling,
One marriage soon gone.

He's coming for us soon, oh so soon.
Let's all be ready.
Soon the trumpet shall sound.
So soon, so soon.
It's sooner than your think.
He's coming, He's coming.

Little Boy

Little boy alone,
No one sees, no one knows,
No one feels what you feel.
Intensity of thought,
Desperation of mind,
Fear.

Little boy, please look up
Through the trees.
See the sun.
See the hope.
See the love.

Fight, little boy
For you are not alone.
The end is not yet
Fight
Fight
Fight

He has seen.

If Ever

If ever I could love you,
I would love you so well.
I'd hold you until all the loneliness
Of all the years was gone.
I'd look into your eyes and
See and understand all that was there.

I'd listen until your words ran dry.
And then I'd be there when the shadows
Began to fall and life found you
Needing a hand to guide you across
The street or a voice to soothe you
If pain should stay.
If ever I could love you,
I would love you so well.

Hope

For Tweety

Her laughter echoed long though sadness lived
Within her eyes. Smiles hid her pain and tears that
Came so easily were quickly covered.

Wounds that could be seen were small
When compared to the greater wounds of the heart.
For as long as she could remember love had hurt
And broken the deepest part of her.

She did what she had to do to survive.
Running in beauty in jeans and t-shirts
Finding comfort and escape outdoors.
Games, 4-wheeling, volleyball anything to
Keep moving and not think, not remember.

She loved her kids intensely with a love she never
Knew herself. They were her world. They gave her a reason
To get up each day, to go to work, to make a different life.
Knowing that in time love given is love returned.
Choosing to believe that tomorrow will be better,
That her hurts will be healed, that there is hope in
Spite of sorrow and that one day she will laugh without tears.

"And now may the God of hope fill you."
Romans 15:13

Father of Love

Father of love, love me tonight.
For only You know the hurts
I carry deep inside.
Only You can heal when
Sorrow lingers long.

Father of Love, love me tonight
For I know that you promised
That you would never leave me.
Only You remain when
All others have gone.

Father of love, love me tonight.

Not Worth the Wait

Oh Mama, he said that I wasn't worth the wait.
Said he had other fields to explore and I
Should go my own way and find someone who
Cared for me in the way I needed.

Oh Mama, I love him! How could he say that?
I thought he loved me too. He said he did.
But now I don't matter and there are others
He wants to know--a life he wants to sow
Without me.

Oh Mama, will the pain ever end?

"Surely He has borne our grief's and carried our sorrows."
Isaiah 53:4

My Love Has Grown Older

My Love has grown older therefore,
I am not afraid of the new wrinkles that
Meet me in the morning mirror nor
Of the pain in my heart when I remember
When we were younger and hopeful of the
Love that would one day be ours for are we
Not closer today that we were then? Has not
Love ripened into a luscious fruit that will
Soon be picked when the time is right?

Meet me when you can and if it must be the grave
Then I will rejoice in the love we will share in another
Land for love cannot die even though miles
Separate our bodies, our souls still live as one.

Every Song I Sing

Playing my songs at night,
Making the people smile
While all the while
I'm hurting deep inside.

Don't know why she left me,
Don't know why it wouldn't work.
Don't know what to do now.
Don't even know where to look.

But honey, every song I sing
I'm singing just for you.
Every smile I smile,
Every tear I cry when I'm
Hurting deep inside is for you.
Just for you.

So tired of the sad game
Of crazy love people play, saying
I love you forever today but
Tomorrow I'm going away.

I want something that's real
Something that will last,
Oh God, show me how to
Hang on to love and hold fast.

Every song I sing is for you, baby.
Every smile I smile
Every tear I cry when I'm
Hurting deep inside is for you.
Just for you.
Don't know why you left me.
Don't know why.
Don't know why you said goodbye
I just wanna sit and cry.
Change me Lord. Please change me.

On Her Good Days

On her good days she would talk and laugh
As though the whole world were a field of flowers
And it was her job to walk barefoot through them.

But on her bad days she would cry
And lock herself inside, away from the faces
And voices and the fields she loved,
Befriending the darkness of her room,
Nursing the emptiness.

He would come then because she asked Him to
And because He knew that He was needed.
He would stay as long as she wanted Him to.
As long as she was willing to walk together
With Him into the loneliness and discover
Again how it came to live so intensely in her
Heart and why some days it refused to leave.

He reminded her that she was special and set apart
And that the last chapter of her life had not yet been read.
But if she could hang on a bit longer she would see
And understand what only He could see now.

On her good days she would talk and laugh
As though the whole world were a field of flowers
And it was her job to walk barefoot through them.

But on her bad days she would cry and lock up
The painful memories of her heart until He came
Along with the key and lovingly opened up the
Sadness with His hope.

The Sunset

The sunset so full and bursting with light
Is cold to me now as I wait for the night to
Cover me and my pain. The emptiness is
Too much to bear for you are not here.

So lonely is the sunset as my heart hurts for what
We had. The moments we sat up late and
Marveled at the world and our love that was
New and bursting with hope for tomorrow.

Now the sunset's colors seem sad and dark.
I can only wait for sleep to numb me for
Awhile. The pain of losing you feels ugly
And not at all what I see in the sky tonight.

I Know Not the Words

I know not the words to tell you how I feel
Except that I love you and my love for you is real.
I know you need to go and see what's out there
But please remember my words.
Remember, that I care.

Remember how we met when we were only ten?
And how we liked to play dress up and pretend
That we were older and could go where we wished?

Somehow we got lost. Somehow we missed holding
On to the most important things like friendship and love
And dreams that we shared that lifted us so far above
All the heartache and fears, the loneliness, the tears.

Somehow, as we grew, we grew away from each other
And now I know not the words to tell you how I feel
Except that I love you and my love for you is real.

Hearts Alive

Hearts alive and softly
Breathing words to songs
That music cannot express.
Beautiful music that soars
Like the eagle, lifting and living
In freedom and hope.

Music that is strong and solid
Standing with eternal love and
Completion.

Music that causes one to laugh,
Rejoicing that he is alive.

Music that hearts alive and breathing
Are not allowed to dance to yet.
Not allowed to feel yet.
Not allowed to sing yet.

Music that is too beautiful, too bright
For this world for there are no notes
To express the deep longing of the soul to be
Totally free to live and breathe
And sing unhindered by darkness.

Music that hearts alive and softly
Breathing will one day know by waiting
On and watching for the One who holds the music,
The words and our every breath.

Hearts alive and breathing.

My Heart is With You

You are gone now. Left at the first ray of light
That shone through your bedroom window.
I am sleeping still in hopes that I might
Find a reason to open my eyes and greet the day
Without you. You left me in the dark with no
Answer to my whys or even a gentle touch to
Remember you by.

Though it may not matter at all to you now
Please know that my heart is still with you,
Beating in the depths of your blue eyes.
My heart is with you no matter how far the miles.
And I would love to be with you if only I could
My prayers today are filled with love.
It's simply understood.
My heart is with you.

You Do Not Walk Alone

There's a sadness in this world today
That feels like it's here to stay.
A hunger that all of us seek to fill,
A thirst that just won't go away.

We party recklessly like there's no tomorrow.
And desperately cry like the pain will always stay.
Where's the hope in all our sorrow?
The sun to light our darkened ways?

For the partying will one day end.
And the tears will all be wiped away.
Hope will live in sorrow's place
And the Son will shine on all one day.

So don't despair, don't give up hope.
Smile, for you do not walk alone.
Place your hand in the One who tread the
Same road and will safely lead you home.

Convent Walls

Convent walls are thick as my heart that must hide.
Lock the doors tight Lord, for I cannot be trusted.
I cannot go and love, forbidden for me. Always.

My tears are many behind my convent walls.
My cries loud yet no one hears.
For this is my sentence alone. So secure
The doors for I would escape if I could.

I see you weeping, my Jesus, in great agony
On your cross, so much heavier to bear than mine.
I know you understand. I die before you on my
Knees in the prime of my desire. Day unto night
You make an end of me.

I have considered the joy of the morning sun
But it does not come. My convent has no windows,
No light, only you Lord to fellowship with in
Suffering. Dreams too vivid of life outside these
Walls mock my reality.

Double lock the doors Lord!
For I cannot be trusted.
I see no deliverance but these walls
To hide my heart from the Land of the Living.

"You will forget the shame of your youth and remember no more the reproach
Of your widowhood for your maker is your husband."
Isaiah 54:4-5

Can't Stop Thinking About You

For Monica

The walls are closing in on me again.
I can't stop thinking about you.
Where you are, what you're doing
Do you know that I still love you?

I heard that you went out with someone new
And just can't believe that it could be
That you're already moving on and
Forgot all the promises you made to me.

I know that I should do the same,
Do what I can to get over the pain.
But what do I do with my broken heart and
The love inside that still remains?

I can't stop thinking about you.
Can't stop. Can't stop.
Can't stop thinking about you.
I love you. I love you.

Maybe you will see me with my friends.
Maybe you'll even see me smile.
But know it's only for a moment
My laughter only lasts a little while.

My heart is falling completely apart.
My mind is far from clear.
I'm longing for you so much.
I'm hurting and wanting you near.

Oh, if you could see yourself the way
I see you; you'd understand what I'm saying.
Look deep into my crying eyes and know
That I'm for real--I'm not just playing.

I can't stop thinking about you.
Can't stop. Can't stop.
Can't stop thinking about you.
I love you. I love you.

When I Am 90 and You Are 91

A poem of friendship for Joanna

When I am 90 and you are 91
We'll waddle the way of friendship
Beneath the noonday sun.

Over tea and cookies and children long grown,
We'll eat the bread of memories and
Reap the seeds we've sown.

A knock may not be heard and
Vision sometimes blurred.
Orange skirt, purple shirt,
Tennis shoes and unseen crumbs
Will it really matter
When you are 90 and I am 91?

When I am 90 and you are 91
The days will pass in wonder
Beneath the setting sun.
Now, did I .....? Can we...?
Where did I put that....?
Will often fill the air.
But we'll not worry or despair for
Memory will find it's way back
In it's perfect time
And we'll see that we lack
Nothing of the things we lost.
For love will be plenty and laughter
Will have won for I am only 90
And you are 91.

Intimacy

From Psalm 139

Oh Lord, you have examined my heart
And know everything about me.
You know when I sit down or stand up.
You know my every thought.

You chart the path ahead of me and
Tell me when to stop and rest
Every moment you know where I am.
You know what I am going to say even
Before I say it. You go before me and
Are behind me. Your loving hand is upon my head.
This is too amazing for me and too
Wonderful to comprehend!
I can never escape from your spirit.
I can never get away from you.

If I go up to Heaven, You are there.
If I go to the place of the dead you are there too.
If I ride the wings of the morning and
Dwell in the deepest ocean, even there your
Hand will guide me and your strength will
Support me. If I ask the darkness to cover me
And the day to become night, even in darkness
I cannot hide from you! To you the night shines as
bright as the day. Darkness and light are both alike to you.

You have made all the delicate inner parts of my body
And knit me together in my mother's womb.
Your workmanship is incredible! You watched me
As I was being made in utter seclusion and woven
Together in the dark of the womb.
You saw me before I was born.
Every day of my life was recorded in your book.
Every moment was laid out before a single day had passed.
Your thoughts towards me Lord are filled with love.
When I sleep you are there. When I wake in the
Morning you are still with me.

I invite you, O my God, to search me and know me.
Show me how you want me to act and think and be.
And lead me always in the path of everlasting life.

Lorene Masters

Loving You Tonight

Trying to stay busy but my thoughts keep on finding you.
Wondering how you're doing and if you're making it through.

I see your sweet face wherever I happen to be.
Praying it won't be long now until it's just you and me.

I'm loving you tonight though I'm loving you alone.
I'm missing you tonight wanting you to come on home.
'Cuz busy's not working when you aren't there and
My heart can't stop hurting until you're home with me here.
I'm loving you tonight.

It's lonely out shopping when you're not in any aisle.
I miss not even talking with you about the weather for a while.
Wishing you never had to go but knowing you miss me too
Keeps me going day by day and keeps away the bad blues.

I'm loving you tonight though I'm loving you alone.
I'm missing you tonight wanting you to come on home.
'Cuz busy's not working when you aren't there and
My heart can't stop hurting until you're home with me here.
I'm loving you tonight.

Darling, let me tell you that I feel like I'm only half a man
Until you walk on through that door and show me you understand.
And just hold me like you do whenever we've been apart too long.
And tell me that your love is just as true as ever, just as strong.

I'm loving you tonight though I'm loving you alone.
I'm missing you tonight wanting you to come on home.
'Cuz busy's not working when you aren't there and
My heart can't stop hurting until you're home with me here.
I'm loving you tonight.

Don't You Hate It

Don't you hate it when people laugh while you cry?
And act like you should know something that you
Have no way of knowing?

Don't you hate it when the walls close in on you
In every room that you are in? And taking a walk
Only postpones the inevitable emotions?

Don't you hate it when the tears just won't stop?
And taking a shower is the only place where you
Don't have to explain them?

Don't you hate it when it seems that no one hears?
And you find yourself alone again with feelings that
Paralyze and overwhelm?

Don't you hate it when you can find no way out
And no way in and no way through? And tomorrow
Feels like it will be as hard as today only worse?

Don't you hate it when people laugh while you cry?

How Loud the Wind Sings

How loud the wind sings when there are no other voices and
Cars and other people noises are lost in another time.

How talkative are the trees when skies are clear and
Birds are the only residents of fresh, blue life above.

How loud the wind sings when it's calling your name
Come away, come away, I'm waiting here for you.

Trail to the top of God's beautiful world —seeing life
Perfect and untouched. Free to sing loudly as the wind calls
And calls....come home...come home...

True Love

I was thinking of you today and thought
That if you only had one arm and one leg
I would still love you and not mind at all
Having to push you around in a wheel chair.

And if you lost your keys or your job or
Your mind, I would stay and help you find
Them. And if your eyes stopped seeing and your
Ears quit hearing and your words no longer
Came, I would teach you how to speak and
Help you to listen by showing you the sound
Of my love.
For love is patient, Love is kind. Love is not jealous
Or boastful or rude. Love does not demand it's own way.
Love is not irritable and keeps no record of when
It has been wronged. Love never gives up, never
Loses faith, is always hopeful and endures
Through everything. Love will last forever.

I was thinking of you today and knew that I
Now know what true love is.

Please Do Not Speak

Please do not speak for I am afraid your words
May hurt me and tell me that things have changed
And you no longer love me. I could not bear
Those words, my love, when my love is the same.

Please do not speak but let me remember how it was
Before, when I was sure of your love and your every
Word filled my heart with joy.

Please do not speak unless you can tell me that you
Love me still and your heart has been steadfast
As mine waiting in silence for this moment.

Please do not speak.

Beautiful Lady

For Robyn

Hey beautiful lady, you're always busy taking
Care of others who need your gentle hand,
While you disregard your worth and worry
If things will turn out as you've planned.

If you would just take a moment to really
See yourself the way we all see you,
In everything you are and all that you do
You really couldn't help but feel beautiful too.

'Cuz mirrors don't show
What's buried deep inside.
But when your heart is in action
It's impossible to be denied.
That you are beautiful, so beautiful
My beautiful lady.
I'm so glad that you are here.
You're beautiful, so beautiful.
Now wipe all those tears 'cuz you are
So beautiful to me.

Day after day you do all that you can to
Keep things together while fighting off the fears
So afraid that it won't matter in the end.
Let me tell you it will; so wipe away those tears.

There's a day coming when we will all reap
The good and the bad from what we've sown.
I want to be there and see your great harvest
From the kindness and love that you have shown.

'Cuz mirrors don't show
What's buried deep inside.
But when your heart is in action
It's impossible to be denied.
That you are beautiful, so beautiful
My beautiful lady.
I'm so glad to have you near.
You're beautiful, so beautiful.
Now wipe all those tears 'cuz you are
So very beautiful to me.

Storm's Passing

Flowing tears run down your face
As your small boat tosses and turns
In raging waters that are much too strong for you.
Wild storms overtake from a cloudless sky.
Shifts in the wind come quickly leaving you cold
And in the dark unable to see what was so clear
Yesterday. Seasons swiftly change and you
Feel alone in currents of confusion and loneliness.

Yet there is One who will send warm winds laden
With hope to calm the fearful heart. Directing the
Battle-weary soul in anticipation of what is to come.
He shall gently lead to safe harbors. In passing by the currents
Of pain that shattered your dreams you will see rose
Petals floating on the now peaceful surface for it is never for nothing
When we love--never is the return empty.
All things are made beautiful in His time--
The broken heart,
The longing unfulfilled,
The loss of someone so loved.

The promise still holds.
Those who weep now will be comforted.
Every tear shall be wiped away.
The former things will pass away.
The new shall come.

What we see now is not all there is.
Quickly can summer be brought out
Of winter. And though springtime was
Spent in sorrow we shall see how the rain
Though cold and unforgiving at the time,
Cleansed our soul and caused us to hope
Not in ourselves but in Him who is far greater
Than the pain of this passing world.
For He has overcome and so shall we.

About the Author

Lorene Masters has loved poetry since her 7th grade English teacher, Mr. Timberman, wrote, "This is beautiful!" on a return poetry assignment. Feeling anything but beautiful at the time, his words would give her hope for years to come.

In addition to writing poetry Lorene is an actress, a dramatist, a radio announcer, and a home school mom. She lives in South Dakota with her husband Dave and their two girls Hannah and Rachel.

Made in the USA
Lexington, KY
14 October 2010